GÉRALD GAMBIER

The traditions of
LYON'S
gastronomy

EDITIONS
LA TAILLANDERIE

PLURIEL

COLLECTION PLURIEL

Edited by Gérald Gambier

Text and
Photographs :

Gérald Gambier

From cover :

*Rue Tupin, Stépharo's warm
chicken liver loaf.*

Infography : Patricia Graizely
Translation : Hedwige West

© Editions La Taillanderie - 2002
rue des Frères-Lumière
01400 Châtillon-sur-Chalaronne
Tél : 04 74 55 16 59

e-mail : editions-la-taillanderie@club-internet.fr
www.la-taillanderie.com

ISBN 2-87629-254-8
ISSN EN COURS

summary

FOOD-LOVER'S MECCA

For all food-lovers, it is in the twentieth century that Lyon came into its true title of glory with the illustrious Curnonsky, pontificating ex cathedra from the famous restaurant Vettard, consecrating the town as '*world capital of gastronomy*' in 1934.

'*Lyon est la capitale mondiale de la gastronomie, car ici la cuisine atteint tout naturellement ce degré suprême de l'art : la simplicité*' (Lyon is the world capital of gastronomy because its cooking has very naturally reached the supreme pinnacle of art : simplicity).

Thirteen years later, in 1947, the same man made this definitive declaration: '*I have had meals in almost every single restaurant in France, and nowhere have I eaten as well as in Lyon. And I don't mean only at the most renowned one hundred or so establishments of the city, about thirty of which enjoy a worldwide reputation, but also in the most modest of inns and in some Lyonnais private homes, where some of my hosts have proven to be veritable guardians of the glories of food*'.

As an integral part of the Lyonnais spirit, the ancestral tradition of good eating had received wide recognition in the nineteenth century when Stendhal's work '*A Tourist's Memoirs*' was published. In it he states: '*I know of one thing which is very well done in Lyon. One can eat there admirably, and I think much better there than in Paris. Vegetables are divinely prepared there… I found that potatoes are prepared in twenty-two different ways, and at least twelve of these are unknown in Paris.*'

The writer Chateaubriand, in 1805, spoke of a place '*where one is fed so prodigiously well that one can barely gather the courage to leave the superb town.*'

Indeed, the history of Lyon itself is that of its cuisine. But such important recognition has to be worked on and cultivated. If in Lyon one is born a food-lover and a gourmet, one's whole attitude and philosophy of life are also paramount, like some kind of wisdom. In his work '*Pleasant Lyonnais Wisdom*', Nizier du Puitspelu claims that '*the table is the place which brings us all together*' and that '*it is better to warm up together at a meal than catch cold working outside.*'

For others, the table is a source of enlightenment for the people. Brillat-Savarin, originally from nearby Bugey but accepted as honorary Lyonnais, goes as far as to affirm that '*the discovery of a new dish is more beneficial to mankind than the discovery of a new star*'. Edouard Herriot, a previous mayor of Lyon, a politician, and a poet, concurred when he said '*in the fragrance of a glass of Beaujolais and in the aroma of a Bresse chicken, isn't there a bit of that "light*

Lyon's indoor market 'les halles' is a veritable institution. One must visit the stall of celebrities like Renée Richard, specialist of the Saint-Marcellin cheese, or Colette Sibila, who is the reference for saucissons.

and winged something" which Plato made the essence of poetry?'

Herriot went on declaring his love for the culinary delights of Lyon – known at the time as *'capitale des gueules'* (food-lovers'Mecca) – and picked up an already popular local maxim: *'Au travail on fait ce qu'on peut, mais à table on se force'* (at work one can only do so much, but in front of a good meal, one has to make an extra effort).

As Henry Clos-Jouve wrote: *'this cult of food is a religion which is peculiar to Lyon. There one finds its assiduous faithful and also its fervent officiants'*. This rather mystical opinion was shared by Léon Albric: *'All religions have eating and drinking as part of their symbolic rituals ; food is thus the base of spiritual life.'* It is not so surprising then that the Lyonnais are great mystics, and that they should have been so well protected by the Virgin Mary in 1643 and in 1870.

Did you know that between the Rhône and the Saône rivers, the advised method of seducing a woman is to take her out to a restaurant on a first date, not to the cinema or a club? Of course, what else could you expect. Lyon is a fortress, a kind of bastion, assaulted by the many products of its neighbouring counties, supported by the interior resistance of its many caterers, restaurants and shopkeepers who win you over as soon as you set foot in town and deliver you defenceless into the hands of gastronomy.

Joseph Berchoux, the inventor of the word *'gastronomy'*, wrote a poem about this very abundance, at the beginning of the nineteenth century.

Would you succeed in the art I profess?
Find then a castle in Auvergne or in Bresse,
Or up on the hills from whence Lyon sees chase
Her two graceful rivers in loving embrace.
That is the place you will find yourself able,
To gather and lay the best fod on your table!

Opposite, an assortment of Lyonnais charcuteries at
Colette Sibila: choice and quality.

HAVE AN OTHER FLICE
OF HISTORY?

The history of Lyon's cuisine starts with the Celtic cult devoted to the sow, whom the druids thought of as an initiation symbol. They depicted it with a distaff, representing the thread of knowledge. But this cult also had secular aspects.

At the Gallo-Roman Museum in Lyon, a tombstone dating from the first century AD represents a typical meal of a roman patrician. Sucking pig and various poultry were washed down with wine from an amphora. The same museum shows the food-oriented views of those times with the pig-shaped weights used to exchange foodstuffs on the markets.

On Fourvière hill, digs have brought to light several tons of oyster shells, impressive evidence of the quantity of those delicacies consumed at the time, and such a long way from the sea! The Romans used them to stuff entire pigs, for their gargantuan parties, together with *'fig-peckers, thrushes and other delicacies'*, cooked in the *'Trojan'* style.

The cured meats of Gaul were already well known at the time of the Roman rule, and many inns in Lyon enjoyed an enviable reputation, as one can see at the Gallo-Roman Museum. The Celts excelled in pork breeding and exported their produce to Rome. Varro, one of Pompey's lieutenants, whose death is recorded in 27 BC, wrote in his Rerum Rusticarum Libri: *'the charcuterie of the Gauls has always been esteemed for its excellence and the quality of its produce. The thriving export trade of their hams, sausages and other similar delicacies to Rome every year prove their superiority as well as their taste.'*

One has to note the use by Varro of the word *'always'*, a good two thousand years ago. That's how ancient the reputation of these products is !

Dried and fresh sausages were the simplest way to preserve this very popular, tasty and cheap meat, but other, rather more elaborate recipes were also popular. The book of the roman Apicius, early in the first century AD, catalogues some of them. One particularly memorable recipe is that of the cold meat pie they used to make out of sow's teats, pike and chicken meat, eggs, pine nuts, fig-peckers all minced together with wine and garum (a macerated mixture of fish entrails and herbs), and finally baked in a pastry shell. Sounds rather tasty.

One can understand why, to the Romans, Lyon was sometimes referred to as *'Copia Augusta'*: the great abundance!

After Antiquity, Lugdunum lived a through a period of rusticity with the barbarian control of the region, but this eclipse ended by the Middle Ages. This was an exceptional period, seeing the creation of Romanesque and Gothic art, and new life breathed into city, just as the basis of the French language was set. Numerous new words appeared then, which are still now synonymous with Lyon and its food.

First, the '*cabarets*'. The term, as early as 1275, referred to any place serving food and drink. Following the roman tradition, each of those places had to display an identifying sign above its door, signalling the sale of alcoholic drinks.

Bacchus being the god of the vine, wine and vegetation in general, the Romans used plants as illustrations for their signs. Ivy was used mainly, but also box, pine and holly. The latter was often hung as a bunch or in a ball above the door.

Some other plants had been considered as sacred and used to represent Bacchus. The thyrse, a long ivy and vine-covered staff ending in the shape of a pine cone, was carried by priestesses during Bacchanalian feasts.

The Gauls, whose town Lugdunum had become the second most important town in the roman Empire, continued this practice until the Middle Ages. So the greenery on the signs of the various eating and drinking places stayed on, and another new word appeared. The word '*bouchon*' comes from the old French word '*bousche*' meaning leaf, foliage or sheaf (when twisted and used as a stopper, it is the ancestor of the cork). Nizier de Puitspelu, in his *Littré de la Grand'Côte*, a dictionary published in 1894, confirmed this etymology and added that just as the cabaret is identified by its sign, the greenery '*bouchon*' gave its name to the restaurant '*bouchon*'.

When the term '*bouchon*' was coined at the end of the thirteenth century, the association with a sheaf of wheat (bousche) was understood : the image of a wheat sheaf hung outside an establishment is one that has been preserved in Lyon's collective memory. At the time, even if the word in itself did not signify an inn, it already could be used to refer to a cabaret by association, perhaps even as a joke.

A few miles from Lyon, a sculpted Bacchus. On a door which might have been that of a cabaret.

Another theory as to the origins of the term '*bouchon*' is that it dates from the end of the fourteenth century, when innkeepers, who offered lodging as well as food, decided to differentiate their signs from those of the cabarets. The richest would have their signs made out of iron, wood or even stone. For the poorest, a simple handful of wheat or grass would suffice. The '*bouchon*' signified the horses' straw and their '*bouchonnée*' (rubbing) as well as their owners' bedding. This hypothesis of illustrated signs can be verified in other towns in France, and for other professions: a wheat sheaf for bakers, apples for cider-makers. Close to the quai Saint-Vincent (the patron saint of wine-makers), rue Bouteille owes its name to the bottle which the owner of a cabaret chose as the sign for his establishment, and the same is true of rue Tavernier.

Still, this typically Lyonnais use of the word '*bouchon*' to describe a restaurant is difficult to place. Etymologists disagree about the source of the word, because nowhere can we find definite proof that inns took this name during the middle ages when the wheat sheaf would signal such an establishment. Even if the association seems to have been created during the middle ages, the word for a Lyonnais restaurant only appeared much later.

Lyon is surprisingly the only French city to use the term exclusively. Can it be that, although the practice was the same all over Gaul, the Lyonnais alone kept the word and its meaning? In the nineteenth century, in Paris, one could still find above restaurant doorways iron-work signs inherited from the eighteenth century fashion of representing vine branches, pine cones and ivy winding round the jovial face of Bacchus. Still, the word did not settle in the language of Parisians or anyone else. While etymologists go on searching, one can but wonder how the bouchon became this modern temple of good fare, with its checked tablecloths and its décor brimming with pictures of the old Lyon, Guignol-related objects and old enamelled signs, where everything predisposes the spirit and the stomach for a rollicking good time in the same way as the interior of a church invites contemplation.

One last thought for what the Middle Ages left us in our gastronomic inheritance. The word '*bacon*', which stands in French for a dried and smoked cut of pork, comes from the Lyon area. Originally '*bakko*' in Frankish, the language of the Francs, it was used from the thirteenth to the sixteenth century, then disappeared from the French language, and resurfaced in the English tongue in 1895.

The Renaissance came to Lyon as to a city of abundance. Its reputation depended to some extent on the Saint-Jean and presqu'île areas, where rich Florentine merchants and bankers would make their tables the celebration of their wealth. Thus, the poet Clément Marot would write : '*a stay in Lyon is sweeter than a hundred maidens*'.

In one of his poems, the Lyonnais Claude Mermet described the use of cardoon and artichoke in sixteenth century cooking. The latter was reputed as an aphrodisiac :

The artichoke, princely artichoke - (L'artichaut, le bel artichaut,)
For the gentleman and for the lady, - (Pour Monsieur et pour Madame,)
Heats the body and the soul, - (Pour échauffer le corps et l'âme,)
But also puts fire in your loins. - (Et pour avoir le cul chaud.)

That rather direct and colourful language was very popular at the time. Just think of Rabelais! His posting as a doctor in the Hôtel-Dieu in Lyon in 1532 seems to have triggered something in the town. He spread around his very peculiar type of joviality linked to wit and his love of food.

Rabelais was greatly inspired by the city, which in turn welcomed his presence at a time of famine and plague. He published his first two novels in Lyon, Pantagruel and Gargantua, two books which depict well the celebrations, the poetic jousting and the excesses of food of the Renaissance in Lyon. One can truthfully assert that Rabelais is responsible for setting the tone of gastronomic excellence in Lyon, toying with dishes as he toyed with words, condemning gluttony and drunkenness as he went.

In his descriptions one finds the fragrance of Old French which bestows a particular savour to food, which it seems to have lost nowadays. Their enumeration alone is poetry to our ears: *'fried tripe and Lyonnais soups* (perhaps the *'gratinée'* or the pumpkin soup), *fine-looking hams and juicy grilled meats*, *'boutarge'* (seasoned smoked mullet roe), *smoked ox tongue, andouille* (seasoned tripe sausage), *'carbonnade'* (the ancestor of barbecue perhaps, or meat cooked in beer), *'cabirotade'* (stewed chicken and other fouls), *'hasterets'* (grilled pork liver), *'hochepot'* (meat and vegetable stew), *'eshinade'* (grilled pork), *'fressurade'* (pan-fried offal), *'galimafré'* (meat stew) *all accompanied by wine and prepared by Myrelanguoy, Fripesauce, Pilleverjus'* (or maybe one of the 156 chefs Rabelais hides in a Trojan sow in the battle of the Andouilles !).

The peak is reached with the pages Rabelais devoted to his parody of medieval battles inspired directly by Lyon's *'charcuterie'*. In the Fourth Book, he paints a battle scene of ferocious blood-sausage and massive saucissons attacking under the orders of colonel Riflandouille et Tailleboudin.

At that time, the inns in Lyon were placed under the patronage of Saint Anthony. They rested on a reputation of good fare and cheap prices, even if one had to share a bed with several other travellers. The great Erasmus could not get over it: *'I cannot understand how those Lyon innkeepers manage to treat one with so much sumptuous comfort so inexpensively. One could think that their aim was the practice of virtuous hospitality, and not making a living'*.

At the start of the sixteenth century, a brotherhood of *'maîtres rôtisseurs et poulaillers'* was formed (the ancestor of our modern day chefs), which counted a mere fifty-three members in 1715. They took pride in the fact that they had introduced the *'Indian cockerel'* known around Europe, the bird which Christopher Columbus had brought back from America and that we now know by the name of turkey. One of those members, Louis Dupré, came to fame as Piraud, *'King of the Rotisseurs'*. He was one of the founding fathers of the Lyonnais school of cookery, with his famous stews, foul and game.

A happy time indeed, to witness the boom of such great establishments. One can still admire the proud sign of one of them, the Outarde d'Or (Golden Bustard), at rue du Bœuf in the Old Town. Sculpted in stone, it depicts the slow Canada goose with the inscription *'Je vaux mieux que tous les gibiers'* (I am better than any game).

It is at this time that the *'limonadiers'* (lemonade makers) appeared, who created a famous liquor: the *'eau d'arquebuse'*. This spirit was originally destined to heal arquebus wounds and is still known today as Arquebuse de l'Hermitage. It might not heal wounds anymore but it still seems to nurse the pangs of a restaurant bill.

*Aquebuse bottle,
the local liqueur.*

9

The Golden Bustard, old sign from a poultry dealer.

When Laurent Mourguet, previously a Canut (silk weaver) turned peddlar, created the puppet character Guignol, little can he have guessed that he would soon become the symbol of thirty thousand weavers on the Croix-Rousse, in daily life and in times of strife. The poor Canut workers, working threads of silk, gold and silver and unable to feed their children, became known as '*ventres creux*' (empty stomachs).

At the inauguration of the statue of Mourguet, the Lyon-born politician Edouard Herriot declared: '*Guignol's food is meagre food: cornflour soup, pork scratchings, fromage fort (macerated cheeses), cervelle de canut (soft cheese), matefaim (apple pancake), and bugnes bought in the street, donkey snout cheese, herrings, rancid butter, tripe and paquets de couenne (pork rind boiled then fried).*'

Yet historian Félix Benoit does not agree: '*If those dishes sound rustic and are cheap to make, they are no 'meagre' food. Guignol and his Canut brothers could hold onto their traditional independence and critical minds thanks to this cheap and nourishing food.*'

The Canut were tenacious and they would not allow the pleasure go out of eating. As Benoit put it as he ate a dandelion salad: '*Donkey snout and other crude cuts, in a spring salad with some grilled bacon, could bring a saint to damnation*'.

In 1848, the Canuts fought not for food but for a better life out of the exploitation they had suffered for years. Various technocratic regulations acted like the straw that broke the camel's back, and the Canut workforce was virtually destroyed. Their food, however, lived on.

The bouchons are now the keepers of the workers' cooking and have used their recipes as the basis of a traditional Lyonnais cuisine, full of charm and quality.

Recette

SALADE DE GROINS D'ÂNE AUX LARDONS
(dandelion salad with bacon)

For 4: 800g dandelion leaves, 1 big garlic clove, 2 thick country bread slices (slightly stale is better), 200g bacon cubes, oil, vinegar, salt and pepper.

- Wash the dandelions carefully and drain them. Place them in a salad bowl with salt and pepper and mix thoroughly;
- rub the garlic over the bread and then cut it into croutons;
- brown the bacon for 5 minutes in some butter, then pour over the salad;
- now brown the bread cubes in the same pan and scatter over the salad as well;
- delaze the pan with two tbsp vinegar and pour over the salad;
- mix and serve straightaway.

Recette

LAMB'S FOOT SALAD

For 2: 2 lamb's feet. Vinaigrette, herbs.

- Cook the meat in a good stock then cut it into small cubes (do not leave any bones);
- prepare a Dijon mustard vinaigrette or a cream dressing;
- mix with the cubes of meat and some herbs.

Recette

PORK RIND PARCELS

For 4: 5 or 6 fresh pork rinds, 2 onions, 2 cloves, 2 carrots, 1l chicken stock, lard, flat leaved parsley, salt and pepper.

- Cut the rinds into strips and tie them up with string into 5 or 6 parcels;
- peel the onions and stick a clove into them;
- peel and chop the carrots thinly;
- in a big pan, place the parcels with the onions, the carrots and cover with stock;
- bring to the boil and simmer for about two and a half hours;
- take out the parcels and drain them;
- heat up a pan and fry the parcels in some lard. Season with salt and pepper;
- chop the parsley and mix into the pan. Serve hot.

Menu of the Mâchon des Amis de Guignol
on February 25th 1922

Dandelion salad with capons and herrings
Scratchings platter
Charcuterie, and pork-rind parcels
China bones etc...
Veal with quenelles

Lyonnais gratin
Roast turkey
Doughnuts
Rougeret, Rigotte and blue cheese
Fruit
Percolated coffee
A jug of Beaujolais per head.

At the time of the Canuts, Anthelme Brillat-Savarin was contributing to the development of the Lyonnais spirit, somewhat like a nineteenth century Rabelais. This magistrate and writer born in Belley in the Ain region, a few dozen miles from Lyon, wrote with a cheerful and easy tone which echoes that of the medical student of the Hotel-Dieu de Lyon, two centuries before him. The evident pleasure he took in relating anecdotes to do with gastronomy, hiding his derision beneath a severe tone, and overlaying serious points with burlesque delivery, made him master of a heroic-comic style very much his

A very Lyonnais menu, that of the banquet for the Friends of Guignol in 1922

Grattons, pork scratchings, forever present as an accompaniment for apéritif in Lyon's homes.

own. His masterpiece, published in 1865, only a year before his death at 71, is entitled, very much in the style of the time, '*La Physiologie du goût ou Méditations sur la gastronomie transcendante*' (the Physiology of Taste or Meditations on Transcendent Gastronomy) and is dedicated to what he described as '*the general principles of gastronomy*'. His so-called Cartesian approach to the fundamental causes of the perception of taste is mainly interesting nowadays for the wit of the chronicles which constitute the bulk of the book, and for the discovery of Gasterea, the Tenth Muse, who presides over the enjoyment of taste.

At the turn of the century, the cuisine of Lyon was to deliver its masterpiece. As direct spiritual descendants of the post-revolution woman, the '*Mères*' (Mothers) appeared and changed the landscape of cooking for ever.

Lyonnais bourgeois cooking, precursor of the Mères'cuisine, was born from the trauma of the blood-baths of the Revolution. The middle-classes, mainly linked to the silk-trade, taking refuge in their comfortable homes, began to meet people at home, doing business even around the dining table. From then on, the wives took over the power from professional cooks and other men in the kitchen, marking the end of the era of the Socratic adage '*art trop important pour le confier aux femmes'* (an art too important to be trusted to women*).

A 'demi-deuil'chicken by Mère Brazier.

With the advent of cast iron stoves which permitted the use of pans, it is with the housewives and hired cooks that the first *'modern'* recipes saw the light. The Lyonnais cooks had a feel for produce and a talent for combination. Cookery books were not available, so they went about keeping their recipes in little school-like copybooks, scrupulously writing down dosage, techniques and teaching their secrets to their daughters.

Recette

DEMI-DEUIL CHICKEN

For 4: 1 good free-range chicken (1,8kg), 1 small truffle, carrots, leeks, little turnips, a piece of muslin or gauze, Dijon mustard, griottes (bitter cherries in vinegar), coarse sea salt.

- Slice the truffle thinly and slide them under the skin of the chicken through small cuts;
- wrap the chicken tightly in the muslin and tie with string;
- place the carrots, leeks, turnips and some salt in a pan of water. Bring to the boil;
- when it has boiled place the chicken in it (water should just about cover it);
- poach for 45 minutes;
- serve with mustard, griottes and coarse sea salt, with rice previously cooked in chicken stock.

Recette

CHICKEN WITH VINEGAR

For 4: 1 free-range chicken (1,4kg) cut into four pieces, 1 tsp oil, 2 crushed garlic cloves, 1 large onion chopped, 2 chopped shallots, 4 tomatoes, 1 tbsp tomato puree, 25cl wine vinegar, 50cl dry white wine (12,5° alcohol), 50cl single cream, 2 stalks of tarragon, thyme, 10cl veal stock, salt and pepper.

- Preparation time : 30 minutes. Cooking time : 45 minutes;
- sweat and brown the meat and the giblets in a pan with a little oil;
- reserve the chicken pieces and add the garlic and the shallots to the pan, sweat without browning;
- add the tomatoes, the flour, and the tomato puree. Mix and add the vinegar, the stock, the tarragon and thyme and season with salt and pepper;
- serve hot.

Recipe from Arlette Hugon
Hugon Bouchon Lyonnais, 12, rue Pizay - 69001 Lyon

Arlette Hugon's chicken in vinegar.

Recette

FOWL POACHED INSIDE A BLADDER

For 6: 1 good free-range chicken weighing about 1,8kg, 1 pork bladder, vinegar, 300g pork mince, 1 bunch of parsley, half a truffle, 100g foie gras, 1 egg, 2 small glaces of brandy, coarse salt, 1 small glass of Madera wine, 2l chicken stock, salt and pepper.

- Leave the bladder to drain in the coarse salt and vinegar overnight;
- the following morning, rinse well and dry;
- leave the chicken in some iced water for 4 hours so it retains its whiteness, reserving its liver;
- mix the pork mince with the minced chicken liver, chopped parsley, minced truffle, crumbed foie gras together and then add the egg and one glass of brandy. Season with salt and pepper and stuff into the chicken. Tie it up;
- pierce the meat through here and there with a needle so the chicken doesn't burst;
- place the chicken inside the bladder with 2 pinches of coarse salt, some pepper, one glass of Madera and one of Brandy. Knot up the bladder hermetically;
- pour the stock into a big pan and bring it to the boil and place the bladder in it. Poach it softly for one and a half hour;
- cut the bladder open as you serve it.

Stendhal tells the story of a meal he had in Lyon in 1838: '*The gentlemen had female cooks, not male. The chief matter was to eat well. If a dish was excellent, one would go about eating it in a religious silence. Moreover, every dish was severely judged and without leniency towards the host. On grand occasions, the cook was called upstairs to be complimented, sometimes not unanimously. I remember the touching sight of one, a big graceless girl of forty, in tears at a kind word said about her duck with olives. Be assured that we will never know that recipe in Paris.*'

Modern cuisine was born, a veritable revolution which allowed the difference between the lords'table and that of the people to be reduced. It would of course not erase social inequality, but it would introduce the pleasure of food even in poor households. Thus, the Canut of the Croix-Rousse would delight in his pork and chicken offal and his soft cheeses because they would be deliciously prepared.

For most cooks, finding work in big bourgeois houses was getting harder, so many Mères started their own business. Mère Fillioux, previously the cook of well-known erudite Gaston Eymard, married a wine merchant and found herself at the stove in her husband's establishment, where she prepared meals like this one, offered in 1910 for the modest price of 3 francs: hors-d'œuvre with local charcuteries, chicken stuffed with truffles, gratin of cray-fish quenelles, warm artichoke hearts with foie-gras, cheeses, ice-cream and desserts with Beaujolais and Châteauneuf-du-Pape wine. This type of meal is still in the tradition of the nineteenth century banquet where a meal could be composed of fifteen dishes.

Mère Brazier's famous artichoke hearts with foie gras.

Recette

ARTICHOKE HEARTS WITH FOIE GRAS

For 4: 4 large artichokes, 300g mixed lettuce (different textures and colours will do well), 4 thick slices of foie gras (goose or duck), vinaigrette dressing.

◆ Pull the stalks off the artichokes, don't cut them. Then, with a very sharp knife, cut the tops off the artichokes with a rotating gesture. Pull off the side leaves. Plunge straight away into some cold water and cook for 15 minutes;
◆ when tey are cooked (a fork will easily go through them) turn the heat off and leave them in their cooking water;
◆ make your dressing and use a little to season the salad;
◆ put the artichoke hearts in to the rest of the vinaigrette;
◆ place the salad on the plates and put one artichoke heart in the center with a slice of foie gras on top;
◆ serve with a slice of toasted bread.

Recipe from Sylvain Gonnet - La Mère Brazier, 12, rue Royale - 69001 Lyon

Bernard Constantin's matelote eel (poached in red wine) from the La Rivoire restaurant.

Some have argued that the Mères always served the same dishes, but one has to remember that their sense of perfection dictated their sticking to what they did best. Mère Filloux alone sacrificed over 500,000 chickens in her time, and with the same small knife too. She used to say to her detractors '*The confection of a dish demands years of experience. I have spent my life making five dishes, so that I know I can prepare them as they should be prepared. I will cook no other recipes*'. And Curnonsky, the first modern food critic and ancestor of our Michelin Guide, added with his legendary verve: '*Their cooking is clear and neat, like a La Fontaine fable or a story by Voltaire*'.

Sylvie Girard, in her book on French cooking, wrote: '*A unique phenomenon in the history of cooking, the Mère era restored the authenticity, the mythical aura and the affective value to the role of the woman in her dimension as provider. The move also institutionalised that role*'.

The first ever Mère, Mère Guy, started the movement when she opened her establishment in 1759.

Eugénie Brazier, who learned with Mère Filloux, was the first ever Lyonnais Mère to receive three Michelin stars in 1933. In fact she received not three but six stars, an exceptional case in the history of gastronomy: three for her restaurant in rue Royale and another three for the one on the Luère.

Skate wing with capers by Loulou Chabanel another Lyonnais tradition.

Her most famous apprentice in 1946 was no other than Paul Bocuse, the seventh Bocuse to own the inn in Collonges. He once declared: '*It is with her that I learned to cook with simplicity, which is not to say with ease! I learned to become demanding about produce. I also learned economy, and most importantly I learned that there can be no success without work. It might sound banal but it is often forgotten.*'

Mère Fillioux, Mère Brazier, but also Bigot, Buisson, Caron, Pompon : these were the names at the head of the movement, followed after the war by Léa, Vittet and André - and always the motto was '*où les choses ont le goût de ce qu'elles sont*' (where everything tastes of what it is).

Marcel Grancher, writer and reporter for the Progrès Newspaper, confirmed this saying in 1932 when he declared that '*these are places in the Lyonnais tradition of simple but exquisite food which has been prepared in the most homely fashion*'.

It was through their generosity and familial simplicity that they came to be called Mères. This loving term also reflects their talent and feel for cooking, which places them at the origins of French Haute Cuisine and the training of great Chefs.

Their children now bear prestigious names, and their work has definitely consecrated France and Lyon in particular in the pantheon of world cuisine.

Recette

TENDRON OF VEAL

For 6: 6 tendrons of veal, 2 onions, 4 cloves of garlic, 3 shallots, 10g oil, 50g flour, veal stock, thyme, 1l dry white wine, 6 fresh tomatoes, 1 tbsp tomato puree, salt and pepper, 1 litre single cream.

• In a first pan, sweat the meat in a little oil then reserve in a large saucepan;
• in the first pan, lightly brown the onions, garlic, shallots, then add the tomatoes and sprinkle with flour;
• pour in the white wine and the stock, season with salt and pepper and add the thyme. Pour into the second pan and simmer for about one and a half hours;
• then, take out the meat and keep warm while you reduce the sauce with the cream for about an hour;
• pass the sauce through a fine sieve and season according to taste;
• serve with fresh pasta.

Recipe from Arlette Hugon - Hugon Bouchon Lyonnais
12, rue Pizay - 69001 Lyon

Recette

VEAL LIVER WITH MUSTARD

Per person: 1 slice of liver, 1 glass of cream, 1 tsp French wine vinegar mustard, 1 glass of white wine, 1 tsp butter, salt and pepper.

• Season the liver and pan fry with the butter according to your taste. Keep warm;
• pour the wine in the pan, add the cream and reduce;
• then stop the heat and add the mustard;
• pass the sauce through a sieve and pour on the liver;
• serve with pommes paillassons (finely shredded potato cakes).

Recette

VEAL ESCALOPE WITH MUSHROOMS

For 4: 4 escalopes (about 140g each), 120g of ceps and bolet mushrooms, 40g butter, flour, 1l double cream, spinach, salt and pepper.

• Wash the mushrooms to get rid of grit and dirt and fry them quickly in the butter. Season and keep aside;
• Flour the meat and slowly cook them in the left-over butter. Clear the fat and add the mushrooms and the cream. Season again;
• Take out the meat when cooked and slightly reduce the sauce before you pour it over the escalopes and serve with a spinach accompaniment.

Blanquette de veau.by Arlette Hugon.

Recette

BLANQUETTE DE VEAU

1,8kg veal (on the bone, ribs or shoulder), 3 onions, 4 cloves of garlic, 1 white base from a leek, 1 bunch of thyme, 1 litre dry white wine (12,5° alcohol), 1/2 litre single cream, 1 lemon, butter, oil, salt, pepper, veal or beef stock, capers.

+ Brown the meat pieces in some butter and oil;
+ add the chopped onions, the crushed garlic, sprinkle with flour and stir until the flour has cooked slightly;
+ add the white wine, a little water, the thyme, then the leek, salt and pepper and the stock;
+ let it simmer for about one hour and a half;
+ take the meat out and keep warm. Add the cream and the lemon cut into halves to the sauce and reduce;
+ pass the sauce through a fine sieve and add a handful of capers;
+ serve with rice or fresh pasta.

Recipe from Arlette Hugon - Hugon Bouchon Lyonnais
12, rue Pizay - 69001 Lyon

At the end of the nineteenth century, the 'halles' (indoor markets) opened, and put an end the dark years for the Canuts. Lyon came into the era of the 'mâchons' and the 'bistrots à mâchon'.

The best definition of the mâchon is that of Félix Benoit: '*the mâchon is no orthodox meal. It is a snack one takes with a few drinks around nine in the morning as a way to fill the morning, or around five in the evening, as one waits for dinner*'.

It relies on some kind of a ceremony which starts with charcuteries: some tender '*rosette*', a wrapped up '*jésus*' sausage, the Lyon '*saucisson*', rolled pork head meat and '*civier*' meat. Then, for those whose hunger has not yet been satisfied, a large bowl of '*grattons*' (pork scratchings) is placed on the counter.

A Guignol show, at the Halles.

In 1638 already, the poet Dulaurier described the peculiar fondness the Lyonnais hold for charcuteries:

The enemy of Ceres, amongst the Pythagoreans,
Would have been put to death and cured
By our Lyonnais, so unimaginable for them
Was the idea of a meal lacking in ham or bacon.

Bistrots have a peculiarly homely feel. Deep in the kitchen, on one side of the stove, a pot of stock patiently simmers sending out fragrant plumes of steam out of the kitchen to engulf the dining-room. As you enter a mâchon in wintertime, you come into a world of fragrances, held close by the steam-covered windows, and two things strike you: first, the strong smell of charcuteries and pork meat in every form, but also the serene, somewhat religious silence which is born of tasting and concentrating on the experience. You will feel you have stepped into a temple of good fare.

Opposite, hot charcuteries from
the Amphytrion, in Saint-Jean.

Recette

TRIPE GRATIN

3 carrot, 2 onions, 1/2l dry white wine, 2,5kg tripe, 1 tbsp tomato puree, 2 tbsp flour, 1kg tomatoes, 1l beef stock, herbes de Provence, 1 clove, two bay leaves, 1 potato, some grated cheese or bread-crumbs.

- In the morning: brown the carrots and the onions in the butter;
- meanwhile cut the tripe in pieces and marinate in the wine;
- add the flour and tomato puree then deglaze with the marinade wine;
- add the chopped tomatoes, the beef stock and the tripe, with some herbs;
- add a clove and two bay leaves, season with salt and pepper and simmer all day long;
- pour the tripe into a oven-proof dish;
- add a sliced potato and top with a little grated gruyere cheese or some bread crumbs if you like it best;
- bake for a few minutes and serve straightaway, in its dish.

Recipe from France Deschamps - Au Petit Bouchon Chez Georges
8, rue du Garet - 69001 Lyon

Recette

LENTIL SALAD

For 4: 350g green lentils, 1 clove of garlic, 2 onions, 25g butter, 1 bouquet garni, 50cl dry white wine, olive oil, xeres vinegar, Dijon mustard, flat leaved parsley, salt and pepper.

- Soak the lentils for an hour in some lukewarm water then drain them;
- melt some butter in a deep pan. Add the halved garlic clove and the chopped onions with the bouquet garni, stir well;
- add the lentils and stir again;
- add the white wine and a glassful of water then bring to a boil. Lower the heat to a simmer, cover and cook for about 40 minutes;
- meanwhile, prepare a vinaigrette with 6 tbsp olive oil, 2 tbsp vinegar, 1 tbsp mutard and season with salt and pepper;
- whisk to emulsify;
- drain the lentils and pour into a bowl. Take out the herbs;
- pour the vinaigrette and add the chopped parsley;
- eat warm or cold.

Opposite, gratin of tripe by France Deschamps, at the Petit Bouchon chez Georges.

The chef lifts the lid off his pot and stirs. Then an indescribable amount of varied comestibles emerges from the magic cauldron as he piles them one by one onto a plate. There you will find '*paquets de couennes*' neatly tied, '*cervelas*' stuffed with truffles or pistachios, unctuous tender ribs, fatty bacon, cured bacon, pig tail and trotters, soft '*sabo-det*' sausage and sometimes the ears or even the whole head. Cured ribs and bacon might well have joined the pot straight out of their brine or dry cure, which will only have added to the flavour of the whole.

And on the side you will get the famous '*clapotons*' and '*béatilles*' salads. The '*clapotons*' are lamb or pig trotters which are marinated, cooked and then boned, and added to eggs, chicken livers, herring filets, and endive or lamb's lettuce. The '*béatilles*' are chicken giblets which are the base of many salads and fricassées, and more famously the '*gâteau de foies*'.

At the end of the nineteenth century then, the cuisine of Lyon took shelter in these bouchons, small establishments for the people, veritable museums where the culinary tradition lived on. Often, bouchons took over older establishments. The bouchon Chez Hugon was originally a '*porte-pot*' inn where one would have bought food and wine to eat and drink elsewhere. It was not until 1937 that the current restaurant was created. Mère Jean was once a grocer's shop, founded in 1923: it was much later that it started serving food. The current owner, Gérard Fassinot, often says that food was sold by the weight at first, just like the ingredients that composed it.

If each period in Lyon's history has been referred to here, it is because every one of them has added a stone to build the temple which is Lyon's cuisine. The cuisine of the bouchons can be seen as heir to

A rather pleasant sign.

Opposite, a 'croustillant', pastry stuffed with meat.

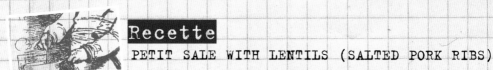

Recette
PETIT SALE WITH LENTILS (SALTED PORK RIBS)

For 8: 3kg salted rib cut, 2 sabodets (pig's head-meat sausage from the Savoie area), 3 carrots, 2 onions, 1 bouquet garni (thyme, bay), 500g small green Puy lentils.

- Cook the meat and sausages with a carrot and an onion in unsalted water. Simmer gently for two to two and a half hours, taking out the sausages after 30 minutes;
- in a pan, sweat two finely chopped carrots and a finely chopped onion in some butter;
- add the lentils and the herbs, stir and add water up to 3cm above the level of the mixture. Slowly simmer until the lentils are soft but retain some bite;
- take out the bouquet garni, add a bit of salt and a good pinch of ground pepper and put the two meats in to warm up together;
- serve hot and sprinkle with parsley.

Recipe from Frédéric Berthod - Brasserie Le Nord - 8, rue Neuve - 69002 Lyon

Recette
LES POMMES PAILLASSON (SHREDDED POTATO CAKES)

For 4: 500g potaoes, 125g butter, salt and ground pepper.

- Peel, wash and dry the potatoes and then grate them not too finely;
- rinse the grated pulp and squeeze it quickly to eliminate most of the water;
- spread the pulp on a thin towel and roll it. Squeeze out the remaining water;
- in a pan melt 40g of butter and pour in the potato pulp in a thick layer, add salt and pepper;
- melt a little butter around the edge of the pan to brown the contour of the cake and leave it to cook for 20 minutes;
- with a wooden spoon, gently lift and turn the paillasson, add 50g butter and let it cook for another 10 minutes or so;
- serve immediately.

Recette
MARROW SALAD

- Blanch the marrow pieces in salted and vinegared water so they firm up;
- quickly fry them in a pan with parsley and garlic and poppy seeds;
- when they start to colour flambé with whisky;
- mix with a little green salad;
- this recipe is given here as an example of typical Lyonnais fare, but the spread of some bovine diseases currently forbids the sale of beef marrow.

The petit salé aux lentilles cooked by Frédéric Berthod.

the cooking of the Mères and that of the Canuts, animated as it is with a will to live on and perpetuate this heritage, getting richer with the passing centuries.

An association was created in March 1997 to bring together some of Lyon's bouchons. They declare themselves: '*anxious to preserve a culinary attitude both turned towards tradition and looking to the future, in an ambiance true to Rabelais's style, dedicated to the freshness and quality of goods from the best producers, and the finest wines France can offer.*'

An authentic Lyonnais Bouchon can be identified by a plaque showing the face of Guignol's friend Gnafron. It proves the owner's commitment to quality in the face of the very prolific tourist traps. Let us commend here the courage and the merit of those who work at preserving the typically Lyonnais culinary traditions. The tablecloth might not always have red and white checks, the owner might often sound a bit rough, but the spirit is more present here than anywhere else.

A number of women work in bouchons, either waiting or cooking, and aware that they are defending the heritage of the Lyonnais Mères. And what is most charming is the great modesty they show before their amazing talent. Let us here mention Arlette Hugon, of the Chez Hugon bouchon, but also France Deschamps, of the Petit Bouchon Chez Georges, Francine Giraud from A Ma Vigne, Brigitte Josserand at the Le Jura bouchon, and at Chez Marcelle, Marcelle Brami, nicknamed '*La Grande Marcelle*': great in talent as well as size.

If the spirit is so particularly strong there, it is because it is being nursed well. Go along to a Beaujolais Nouveau evening at a bouchon, and see if you don't learn something. A diner

29

Rue Garet:
- The little bouchon Chez Georges;
- Le Garet, under the figure of Guignol one can see the plaque which is awarded to 'Authentic' Bouchons

at a neighbouring table may take you aside and ask if you know what '*grisouilles*' are. You will be told of many saucy ways of catching the aforementioned '*grisouilles*', amidst the hilarity of all the other diners. That's the Bouchon spirit. It comes as no surprise that a band of jolly Bouchon fans felt the need to create a society of eaters and drinkers, known as the '*Francs Mâchons*' (a pun on the French for Freemasons). For, as Pierre Grison puts it so well: '*The motto of the Authentiques Bouchons Lyonnais – whether the party-poopers like it or not – is: 'Enjoy your Food, Drink Up, Drink Up !*' (Bon appétit et large soif).

Created in 1964, at the Petit Bouchon Chez Georges, the equivalent of a Nobel prize for Lyonnais wine and food is awarded to restauranteurs who defend the most authentic Lyonnais cuisine: the '*Ordre du Mérite de Gnafron*'.

But to be fair, one has to note that lacking membership to the Authentiques does not take away the savoir-faire, quality and conviviality of other Lyonnais bouchons, which might have decided against being a part of the official association for some reason.

Other Authentiques where the spirit of the Mères is kept alive : *rue des Marronniers and the Meunière, rue Neuve.*

PORK IN ALL ITS STATES

The authentic Saucisson de Lyon.

Grimod de la Reynière, author of the '*Manuel des Amphitryons*' and the '*Almanach des Gourmands*', two publications for food-lovers, declaimed loud and clear his opinion: '*And on the subject of charcutiers, what a very commendable profession that is. And if the Rhône area's pork is better than the Seine's, and if Lyon saucisson is better Paris saucisson, well, that's nobody's fault.*' So true, and for all time!

In a mâchon the star of the show will be some hot pork-related goodie. Still, the saucisson is the all round favourite when it comes to food in Lyon.

Beef did get used once in the making of saucisson, but contrary to popular belief it has never contained any donkey meat. There is as little donkey as there is lion in a saucisson from Lyon. The mistake must stem from a confusion with the saucisson d'Arles, which has similar presentation and was at one time allowed to contain mule, donkey, horse or goat.

Or perhaps a phonetic error was the source of the mistake. The similarity between the sound of '*Arles*' and '*Ane*' could have been it. One can imagine a very busy stall in the Lyon indoor market, the cries and shouts, and dear old Mrs Cotivet, whose hearing is not what it was, asking in a shaky voice:

'*Qu'est-ce que c'est ?*' (What is this?)

'*Du saucisson d'Arles madame Cotivet !*' (Some Arles saucisson, Mrs C)

'*Ah ! Du saucisson d'âne, pauvre bête.*' (Donkey sausage! Poor thing.)

Sabodets and other cooking saucissons. One has to be an expert to see which is which, but the tastes are very different !

Saucisson of Lyon! A poem, a legend!
A jewel of taste whose slices shine
With garnet and specks of white
It opens our feats with rich delights.
Welcomed as a beloved adoptive son
At Lyon's table in warm celebration
This delectable candle comes from afar
Saint-Symphorien-sur-Coise and Chazelle first saw
Its rejuvenating flesh, so charming and so fine.

A varied array of charcuteries Targe.

Recette

WARM SAUCISSON BEAUJOLAIS STYLE

For 6: 1 saucisson for cooking (800g to 1 kg), 1 bouquet garni, 100g shallots, butter, small white onions, button mushrooms, salt and pepper and 1l of Beaujolais

- Sweat the chopped shallots in butter then pour the wine in;
- softly simmer for 10 minutes;
- add the sausage with the herbs and cook for another 20 to 25 minutes;
- take out the saucisson and the bouquet garni;
- reduce the liquid by half;
- dress the sausage peeled and sliced not too thinly onto a serving dish;
- lightly emulsify the sauce with a little brown stock or manié butter;
- sauté the mushrooms and the onions in some butter until they caramelise slightly then add to the sauce;
- add the saucisson;
- simmer for another minute or so and serve with steamed or baked potatoes with a sprinkling of parsley.

Recette

THREE LOCAL SAUCISSONS

- Take three types of cooking sausages (normal – with truffles – with pistachios);
- put them in a pan of cold water and cook them slowly for 40 minutes
- add peeled potatoes. When the potatoes are cooked so are the saucissons;
- melt 200g of butter and add some pistachios, some truffle pieces and pour over the sliced saucissons and the potatoes.

Opposite, the three saucissons of Loulou Chabanel.

Well, Guignol enthusiasts might smile at this facetious explanation, you never know.

Modern techniques may well have improved, but the basic idea is the same as far as saucisson is concerned. Composed of 100% pork or a mixture of pork and up to 25% beef, its quality comes from that of the meat. The guidelines used by charcutiers define it thus: *'the mince has to be a fine and homogenous mince with bigger, square pieces of fat'*.

The real saucisson de Lyon is wrapped in silver paper and slid into a string bag. Only then does it warrant its name and reputation; such a reputation that at the beginning of the twentieth century, Amédée Matagrin dedicated a poem to its origins (see page 33).

Jean-Robert Pitte also paid homage to this delicacy as an object of veneration for Lyonnais food-lovers, quoting this poem by Romain Coolus:

Vivent, sapide Lyon,
Ces merveilles éternelles :
Ton saucisson... de lion,
Ton gras-double et tes quenelles !

Long live tasty Lyon
And your eternal marvels
Your saucisson made of... Lyon,
Your tripe and your quenelles !

It is worth mentioning that the word saucisson, or saulcisson, was coined by Rabelais who translated it from the Italian *'salsiccione'*, itself derived from the Latin *'salsicius'* (salted), around 1546.

The *'rosette'*, or *'fuseau'* (spindle), gets its name from the section of intestine from which its casing is made: it is the last part, ending with the anus: a pink rosette. A large sausage of more than 300 grams, and slightly conical, it is made from lean cuts and not much fat, the whole being coarsely minced to six millimetres. It must be tied inside a natural casing, which is either whole or has been sown onto a cone to retain its conical shape; it can also be strung by hand. The rosette is long and, like a good wine, improves with age.

Bigger still because of the size of casing used, the *'jésus'* sausage can reach up to eight

Rosettes de Lyon and truffled cervelas ; Easy to differenciate.

kilogrammes. Its minimum diameter is 7 cm and ends in an S-bend. It takes its name from the plump shape it takes when tied, by analogy with the shape of a swaddled baby Jesus figure in paintings by Georges de La Tour. The drying process is a crucial element of its manufacture, having great influence on its particular taste and texture.

The cervelas was well known in Rome in Julius Caesar's time. It owes its name to the brain meat, *'cervelle'*, which was added to the bacon and shoulder of pork in the ancient recipe. Lyon's cervelas, pure pork, is also made with natural casing, and is generally stuffed with pistachios or truffles. Despite its simplicity and ease of preparation (poached in water then served with potatoes), it makes a surprisingly festive meal.

The *'saucisson à cuire'* (cooking sausage) is chopped more finely than the cervelas and also contains less fat. It can be poached, boiled or baked, singly or stuffed into brioche dough.

The *'sabodet'*, a real speciality, is a large *'saucisson à cuire'* made with pork head meat, tongue included, with pork rinds and meat which has been generously baptised with spirit and red wine. It is eaten in thick slices with an accompaniment, or at the bar, cut into cubes and served warm as a flavoursome snack.

Amongst Lyon's specialities, the '*grattons*' are some of the most popular. It is a by-product of making lard: the sliced pork skin is cut into strips and once the fat has been melted off, the pieces of skin are pressed and seasoned with salt, pepper and vinegar. At aperitif time, or perhaps while waiting for a table, a big bowlful of grattons will be shared between prospective diners as they chat and put the world to rights.

The andouillette lyonnaise is the second most famous of Lyon's specialities, but beware of fakes and imitations! The true andouillette is composed of pure calf's caul and is stuffed into veal casing. None of that rather smelly pork casing which is used in other regions. On the subject of smell, Edouard Herriot never failed to remind people that '*l'andouillette c'est comme la politique, ça sent toujours un peu la merde*' (an andouillette is a bit like politics, it always rather smells of sh*t). The calf caul is washed and the fat removed, then cut into pieces and marinated before being forced into its casing and rolled in breadcrumbs. For the cooking, the andouillette is basted in red or white beaujolais, then baked. Unfortunately, the bovine diseases of the end of the twentieth century have temporarily made it impossible to use calf's caul. Charcutiers have instead had to revert to pork.

'*Gras-double*' is a type of tripe from one pocket of the calf's stomach. It is diced and fried with a lot of onions and served warm or with salad.

The '*tablier de sapeur*' (sapper's apron) comes from the same pocket of the calf's stomach. It was named by the maréchal de Castellane, governor of Lyon under Napoléon III, who saw in it the shape of his soldiers' aprons. Its preparation starts with marinating, then it is breaded and pan-fried. It is then served with a sauce made with the marinade.

A polemical food if ever there was one, the quenelle is one of the most famous specialities of the area. First there is the name. Some attribute it to the Anglo-Saxon 'knyll' which means pound or crush ; others to the German word for a ball of dough, '*knödel*', or the Alsatian '*kneppfle*' meaning small sausage. But why look so far afield, when the word looks like it might well have been coined here? Rabelais, in 1552, in his Fourth Book, talks of '*friquenelles*': balls of mince.

Recette

TRIPE

For 4: 10cl wine vinegar, 2 nice slabs of tripe, 2 big onions, 25cl oil (peanut, sunflower or grapeseed), salt and pepper, 20cl good dry white wine, parsley.

- Thinly slice the tripe and the onions;
- heat up the oil in a large pan and fry the onions and the tripe on a high heat, stirring often for 20 minutes;
- take off the heat and reserve. Preheat the oven on 180 °C (gas mark 5);
- deglaze the pan with the white wine;
- place the tripe mixture into a gratin dish with the parsley, pour on the vinegar then the deglazing liquid. Bake for about thirty minutes.

Opposite, the Café des Fédérations's tripe.

Recette

WARM CHICKEN LIVER LOAF

For 6: 450g chicken livers, 4 slices of bread, 4 eggs, 4 garlic cloves, parsley, 1/2l milk, 50g flour, 50g butter.

- Mince the livers with the parsley and the garlic;
- make a white sauce and add the egg yolks, the bread (previously soaked in the milk then drained), the liver mixture and salt and pepper;
- whisk the egg whites and carefully add to the mixture;
- pour into a buttered tin then cook in a bain-marie for 35 minutes in a medium oven;
- the loaf is served with a cream sauce (béchamel or nantua) with some pikequenelles.

Opposite, liver loaf from the Stépharo, rue Tupin.

Recette

LE TABLIER DE SAPEUR ('SAPPER'S APRON')

The French name for the appropriate part of the beef's stomach used here is the 'bonnet' because it has the shape of a hat.

+ Cut the piece into steak pieces (about 200g);
+ macerate them in some white wine, some vinegar and salt and pepper for two days;
+ boil the marinade down and add some cream;
+ dry off the aprons, dip them in egg and then into some breadcrumbs or seasoned flour;
+ fry them slowly in some oil and butter till they are golden brown. Be careful not to cook them too fast so they don't become tough;
+ serve on hot plates with sauce and some chives.

Recette

CALF'S CAUL

+ Blanch the cauls for ten minutes in salted water with a dash of vinegar;
+ quickly seize them in a pan with some minced onions and chopped tomatoes;
+ towards the end of the cooking, add a little uncooked tomatoes and sprinkle with poppy seeds, salt and pepper and four spice;
+ flambé with whisky and serve very hot.

Recipe from Jean-Pierre Duplouy - Restaurant La Bressane
2, rue de Cuire - 69004 Lyon

Calf's caul cooked by J. P. Duplouy.

Opposite, a tablier de sapeur

Cooked in white or red wine, grilled, whole or split, the andouillette is always a treat.

Recette

ANDOUILLETTE BEAUJOLAISE

♦ Brown the tripe sausage with some shallots, don't let them burn;
♦ add salt, pepper and 4 spices;
♦ deglaze with Beaujolais wine and reduce. Add a bit more wine and serve

Recipe from Jean-Pierre Duplouy - Restaurant La Bressane - 2, rue de Cuire - 69004 Lyon

Recette

ANDOUILLETTES WITH DRY WHITE WINE

♦ Place the andouillettes in an oven dish and pour the wine half way up the sausages;
♦ Dot with knobs of butter;
♦ Bake in the oven for one hour;
♦ Turn the andouillettes from time to time so they brown evenly.

Opposite, a fragant andouillette from the Stépharo, rue Tupin.

The quenelle was created in the fourteenth century in Nantua, in the neighbouring Ain department, where researchers have discovered documented proof of its invention. It was rapidly adopted in Lyon where it enjoyed a constant popularity. It might not, though, have looked very much like its modern version.

The recipe, too, is a mine-field. Everyone agrees that pike is its basic ingredient but beyond that, opinions diverge. What are the other ingredients? It seems to be a matter of personal preference: crème fraîche, beef marrow, beef dripping, white sauce or choux pastry, and an egg or two to hold it all together. Whichever recipe you chose to follow, the idea is to balance the light moist fish meat with some beef fat and leave a third of the end weight for white sauce or choux pastry. Every cook seems to cherish a more or less traditional recipe in order to obtain the desired lightness, smoothness and taste. Specialists such as Jean Vettard, friend and colleague of Curnonsky, have opted for a white sauce base. The recipe must have pleased the public for Vettard's quenelles were renowned well beyond Eastern France. For chef Matthieu Varille, you need *'one third pike or other fish meat, one third beef marrow or dripping and one third choux pastry'*. Others use far more fish meat. Today, the best chefs and caterers use white sauce, dripping and 22 to 30% pike meat. Others turn it into some kind of soufflé, which is easily recognised after poaching or baking: the soufflé falls and shrinks as it cools, the real quenelle does not.

Regional Queen, the quenelle was served to heads of states at the G7 in Lyon.

Opposite, the succulent quenelle with Nantua sauce
from the Jardin de Berthe, rue Fleurieu.

PIKE QUENELLES WITH CRAYFISH COULIS

Ingredients for the quenelles: *500g pike meat, 200g butter, 6 eggs, 200g flour, 1/2l milk, salt and cayenne pepper.*

Ingredients crayfish coulis: *300g crayfish, crème fraîche, 2 chopped shallots, 2 cloves of garlic, 2 chopped onions, 2 chopped carrots, 1 glass of dry white wine, 1 glass of brandy, tomato puree, 1l fish stock, salt and pepper.*

Quenelles:
+ Finely mince the pike meat and pass it through a fine sieve to reserve any bone;
+ make a panade (melt the butter, add the flour and the salt and pepper. Pour the lukewarm milk in and stir with a wooden spoon to dry off the mixture into a thick paste). Let it cool down;
+ whisk the fish puree and the panade, then add the eggs. Roll the quenelles on a lightly floured work surface, then poach them in simmering salted water for 15 to 20 minutes.

Crayfish coulis:
+ Gently fry the crayfish in a little olive oil with the shallots, the onion, garlic and the carrots;
+ deglaze with the brandy and the wine. Season;
+ add 2 tbsp tomato puree and simmer for 5 minutes;
+ get the crayfish out and reserve the liquid;
+ keep a few crayfish whole for garnish, get the meat out of the rest. Crush the carcasses up with a pestle and mortar together with the bones from the pike, the crayfish cooking liquid and 1l fish stock. Cook for about 2 hours;
+ pass the sauce through a fine sieve, add 4 tbsp of creram and let it reduce slowly.

Dress the quenelles on a plate and pour the sauce over them, adding the reserved crayfish on the side.

Variant : instead of the coulis, one can use lobster bisque.
+ Simmer 30cl cream with 800g lobster bisque and a splash of brandy. Pour the sauce in a deep dish and add the quenelles (the sauce must come up to 3/4 of the quenelles);
+ put in a medium oven (160 °C- 170 °C) for about 20 minutes;
+ serve at once.

GRATIN OF CRAYFISH TAILS

Ingrédients for 1 portion: *20 crayfish, crayfish butter, brandy, cream, salt and pepper.*

+ Poach the crayfish for 5 minutes;
+ drain the tails and quickly fry them in a teaspoonful of crayfish butter;
+ deglaze with brandy, add a ladleful of cream, reduce and season;
+ one can add a hollandaise sauce or glaze in an oven or under the grill;
+ serve with a crisp, cold Bugey Chardonnay and a garnish of leaves.

For reasons of commercial diversity, some quenelles are now made with chicken or turkey, or with veal instead of pike. Some plain quenelles are also stuffed with chopped morrels, prawns or crayfish.

Back in the nineteenth century, originality came in the shape of the famous '*tétons de Vénus*' which Mère Brigousse served in the 1830's and 50's for special requests, like stag parties: these were gigantic breast-shaped quenelles.

The best accompaniment for the divine quenelle is the Nantua sauce, invented in the town of the same name, which has a crayfish butter base. In Lyon, quenelles are also served as a gratin, or with chicken livers from the Bresse area. Ah, blessed county!

Last but not least, two vegetables are said to be peculiar to the Lyonnais cuisine: the cardoon and the onion. Cardoons are truly characteristic. But the tendency to call any onion-based dish '*Lyonnais*' is thoroughly unfounded. Onions do come in the preparation of sauce Lyonnaise, Lyonnais tripe, and the gratinée, which is an onion soup, but are not used heavily in other Lyonnais recipes.

Recette

LES DOIGTS-DE-MORT À LA LYONNAISE
(death's fingers salsify Lyon style)

For 4: 800g salsify, 1 tbsp butter, parsley, chives, 1 shallot, 1 clove of garlic.

+ Clean and wash the salsify and boil them for 15 minutes. Let them cool, dry them then dress them in a dish which will stay in the oven while the sauce is being prepared;
+ put the chopped herbs (reserving a sprig of parsley), shallot and the whole clove of garlic in a saucepan with the butter;
+ sprinkle with flour and heat up;
+ add the cream and let it simmer for 15 minutes. Sieve the sauce;
+ when ready to serve, warm up again with a little butter and finely chopped blanched parsley to the sauce. Season with salt and pepper;
+ pour the sauce over the vegetables. Eat warm.

The cardoon was already cultivated by the Romans, and this sensitive vegetable is a common sight in the sandy fields of Val de Saône, between Belleville and Lyon, neatly wrapped for protection and blanching. It was served at Louis XIV's table together with quenelles. They are transplanted on St Georges'day and the hearts and stalks are collected from October until April.

Preparation of the cardoon requires some patience and abnegation. After peeling off the stringy outer layer, the stalks are diced and quickly plunged into milk and water to prevent them from oxidizing. The peeler's fingers on the other hand are stained black. There are not many recipes for this vegetable, but the uncontested best is the sublime 'gratin de cardon à la moelle' (cardoon and beef-marrow gratin). Absolutely wonderful!

There are also some vegetables whose name in Lyon is truly unusual. 'Dents de lion' (lion's teeth), also called 'groins d'âne' (donkey snout) or 'barabans', are of course dandelions. They are eaten in a salad with bacon, hard-boiled eggs and herring, or with crunchy fried pig's ear.

'Truffes' in Lyonnais vocabulary actually mean potatoes, and 'doigts-de-morts' (deadmen's fingers) are not as macabre as they sound : peeled salsify. 'Caviar', of course, is consumed by the ladleful – but as a salad, or with a bit of braised pork, because it actually refers to Puy lentils. 'Blette' or 'joutte' is swiss chard, particularly the 'Ampuis'variety, and finally carrots are called 'racine jaune' (yellow root).

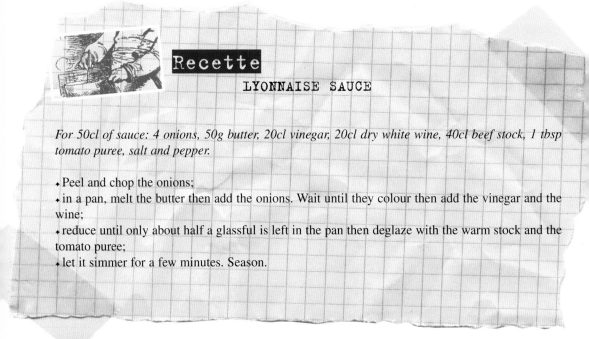

Recette

LYONNAISE SAUCE

For 50cl of sauce: 4 onions, 50g butter, 20cl vinegar, 20cl dry white wine, 40cl beef stock, 1 tbsp tomato puree, salt and pepper.

- Peel and chop the onions;
- in a pan, melt the butter then add the onions. Wait until they colour then add the vinegar and the wine;
- reduce until only about half a glassful is left in the pan then deglaze with the warm stock and the tomato puree;
- let it simmer for a few minutes. Season.

Wrapped-up cardoons in a field of the Val-de-Saône

Recette

CARDOONS WITH BONE MARROW

For 6: 2 big cardoon feet, 60g butter, 150g beef marrow, 1 bunch of chives, salt and white pepper.

♦ Discard the tops and keep only the stalks of the cardoon which you cut into chunks and leave in a bowl of milk and water;
♦ wet some flour in some cold water and add it to 2.5 litres of water in a big saucepan. Bring it to the boil, whisking regularly, then add the cardoons;
♦ cover and leave to simmer for 45 minutes then drain;
♦ melt the butter in a pan and add the cardoons, stir for ten minutes or so, season;
♦ meanwhile, cut the marrow into thick slices and poach them for 3 minutes, then drain;
♦ place the cardoon in a deep dish and add the marrow slices on top;
♦ finish off with chopped chives and heat up in a hot oven for 15 minutes.

Recette

ONION GRATIN SOUP

For 8: 200g finely chopped onions, 50g butter, 75g grated gruyere cheese, 50g flour, 1 head of garlic, 5 egg yolks, 1/2l dry white wine, 1,5l stock, 1 French stick, 1 glass of Madeira wine.

+ Slowly sweat the onions with the garlic in the butter. When they turn golden sprinkle in the flour;
+ let the flour turn light brown then pour on the white wine and the stock (or the same amount of water);
+ season and leave to simmer for 15 minutes;
+ prepare some lightly toasted slices of French bread;
+ pour the potage into a soup bowl which will withstand the heat of the oven;
+ slide the toast on the soup. Sprinkle with the cheese;
+ grill in the oven;
+ when nicely brown, add the egg yolks and the Madeira to the soup;
+ serve boiling hot.

The traditional onion soup, best hang-over cure there is!

A LITTLE SPOT OF CHEESE

Are there any truly Lyonnais cheeses? Indeed there are. Cheeses are perhaps not usually associated with Lyon, and it might surprise some to discover that there are six or seven cheeses representing the area on the French national cheese-board. Two of these are particularly original and poetic: the Sans-Souci cheeses. They are made in the eponymous area of Sans-Souci, in Lyon's third arrondissement. Cheese-maker Jules Ravassard created in 1946 the '*Gros Roman de Sans-Souci*' and the '*Régal de Sans-Souci*'. Taken over by Georges Garnier in 1995, the same fromagerie still makes the two cheeses, quite similar to Saint-Marcellin but bigger, 550g and 200g respectively. They are soft cheeses, matured in a very humid environment which gives them a thick, downy, slightly bluish skin. Their total annual production reaches 40,000 tonnes.

At the fromagerie in Sans-Souci, in the third 'arrondissement', the 'Régals de Sans-Souci' are set in a ladle.

But tradition honours the *'fromage fort'* (strong cheese) best. It is a particular mixture of mature cheeses which have marinated in leek stock and white wine in an earthenware pot. Also a must is the *'Cervelle de Canuts'*. It is an almost mythical food, which stunned nineteenth century writers with its constant consumption in ever Canut home, as an accompaniment for every course.

The Saint-Félicien was created in Lyon in 1954 by a local cheese maker called Bouchet. It is best eaten when it has matured to a runny centre. The Ardèche region nowadays boasts of its production but its origin and biggest consumer base remain in Lyon.

The Lyonnais *'rigotte'* (not to be confused with the Condrieux rigotte) is a small goat cheese which is as good fresh as mature. Likewise for Saint-Marcelin, a cow's milk cheese which is specially matured and a particular favourite for its distinctive taste.

The cheese platter from the fromagerie in Sans-Souci : the 'Gros Romans', the 'Régal' matured twice, the Lyonnais 'Rigotte', the 'Saint-Félicien', the 'Saint-Marcelin', the 'Lyon' matured in white wine and the 'Lyon' matured in spirit.

Maturing of the 'Gros Romans' in Sans-Souci, created after demand by specialists, adds a sweeter and more polished note to the cheese.

The Cervelle de Canuts from Café des Fédérations .

Recette

LA CERVELLE DE CANUTS
('CANUTS'BRAIN' SEASONED SOFT CHEESE)

The cervelle de Canuts, (after a recipe from the nineteenth century.)

For 2: take two well drained soft cheeses. Beat them well to obtain a very creamy texture. Add a splash of vinegar, 10cl of roasted soy oil, 1 big sliced shallot, 15g of chopped chives, 5cl dry white wine, salt and pepper to taste and a good spoonful of crème fraîche. If you like it (and if you have no romantic date that evening), you can add a small amount of crushed garlic. Then again, you might be eating it together… Beat the mixture well before pouring it into the serving dish, sprinkling parsley and chives. Serve very cold with a good Beaujolais.

Bugnes, papillotes and other sweets

Bugnes, very distinctive lozenge-shaped doughnuts, were invented in the sixteenth century by the canoness order of Saint Peter. They used to flavour them with rose water, which has now been replaced by orange-flower water. The recipe was adopted by the *'bugnetiers'* and *'friteurs'* (doughnut-makers and fryers) in the eighteenth century. The original recipe only consisted of a mixture of yeast and flour, but it has now been improved with eggs, milk and butter, and sometimes does not even contain any yeast.

A lot of nonsense has been spread on the subject of bugnes, much of which relates to their status as Lent food. Their original ingredients allowed them to be consumed during Advent and during Lent. And so they stayed for that purpose, but when eaten at other times of the year and Sundays during Lent, their fat content (and their palatability) was increased dramatically. The adaptation of the original recipe must have occurred well before 1873. *'Mardi gras'* (Shrove Tuesday) is the traditional evening when children and adults alike are permitted the excesses of *'gras'* (fat), and bugnes are the popular choice in the Lyon area. Their recipe has a few variations. The most important quality is lightness, as illustrated in this slightly irreverent saying about a 'good' person: *'Celui-là quand il mourra, il est sûr que son âme montera au ciel droit comme une bugne'* (When he dies, his soul will float straight up into heaven like a bugne).

Matefaims (literally, hunger-checkers) are aptly named: they are thick pancakes stuffed with dried or fresh fruits, like apples or pears. There used to be savoury ones as well, with bacon or potatoes, a favourite of the Canuts.

What about *'papillotes'*? Another Lyonnais idea which is linked to a lovely story. M. Papillot, confectioner in the rue Bât-d'Argent at the end of the eighteenth century, had a lovesick apprentice. The young man would steal chocolates and sweets and wrap them up in a love note to give to his sweetheart. M. Papillot caught him and fired the poor man, but the idea was exploited and 'papillotes' were born. They are chocolates or fruit pastes wrapped in

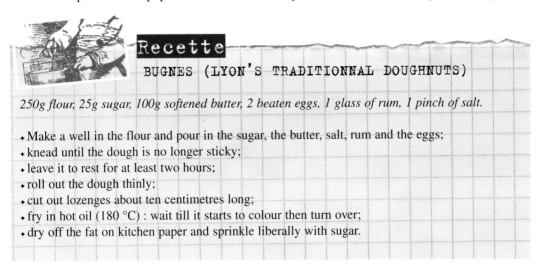

Recette

BUGNES (LYON'S TRADITIONNAL DOUGHNUTS)

250g flour, 25g sugar, 100g softened butter, 2 beaten eggs, 1 glass of rum, 1 pinch of salt.

- Make a well in the flour and pour in the sugar, the butter, salt, rum and the eggs;
- knead until the dough is no longer sticky;
- leave it to rest for at least two hours;
- roll out the dough thinly;
- cut out lozenges about ten centimetres long;
- fry in hot oil (180 °C) : wait till it starts to colour then turn over;
- dry off the fat on kitchen paper and sprinkle liberally with sugar.

Bugnes and waffles by Pierre-Franck Salamon.

a piece of paper printed with a joke or story, then wrapped in a second layer of colourful paper. Historians, contradicting the legend as they always must, claim that the word actually came from the word '*papillon*' (butterfly), in reference to the shape of the bright fringed wrappings.

In the area of sweets, two more modern specialities should be mentioned : the '*coussin*' (cushion) and the '*cocon*' (cocoon). The idea for the '*coussin*' came from the procession made by the town's aldermen in 1643. They placed a golden coin and a seven-pound wax candle on a silk cushion and processed through the town to invoke the protection of the Virgin Mary against the plague. In 1960, the confectioner Voisin created this sweet, composed of chocolate cream and curaçao liqueur, wrapped in green marzipan and crystallised sugar, flavoured with curaçao.

Apple tart by France Deschamps.

The '*cocon*' was created to commemorate Lyon's past and present silk industry. The mayor Edouard Herriot asked one of France's best confectioners, Jean Auberger, to invent a

59

Recette

APPLE TART

4 Golden Delicious apples, 4 tbsp sugar, 150g butter. Pastry case: 250g flour, 1 egg, 1 tbsp sugar, 1/2l water and milk.

- Mix the pastry dough and roll it out very thinly, place it into the tin and use a fork to pierce it at regular intervals;
- finely slice the apples and place them into the case, very tightly;
- sprinkle with the sugar and add the butter in small dots on the apples;
- bake in a moderate oven for 45 minutes;
- take the tart out of its tin staight away. Eat warm or cold.

Recipe from France Deschamps - Au petit bouchon Chez Georges - 8, rue des Garets - 69001 Lyon

Recette

ACACIA DOUGHNUTS

For 3: 125g flour, 1 egg, 1 pinch of salt, 2 tbsp melted butter, 10cl beer, 10cl water, 300g acacia flowers, 150g sugar, white rum.

- Mix the flour, egg yolk, salt, butter, beer and water;
- leave the mixture to rest in a warm place;
- wash the acacia flowers and discard their green stalks. Sprinkle sugar and rum over them;
- leave it to macerate for 2 hours;
- whisk the egg white and add it to the dough;
- dip the flowers into the mixture and gently shake off the excess;
- fry the doughnuts a spoonful at a time;
- dry them onto kitchen paper and sprinkle them with sugar. Serve warm.

Recette

MATEFAIMS

For 4: 2 crisp apples, 150g flour, 2 eggs, 100g sugar, 50g butter, 15cl milk, salt. (Optional : 1 lemon, 2cl pear alcohol or Calvados)

- Peel the apples and dice them up. Add the lemon zest and half the lemon juice (if using) and let it soak;
- Separate the eggs and whisk the whites until quite firm with a pinch of salt;
- Sieve the flour into a bowl and add the yolks and the sugar;
- Progressively add the milk then the alcohol if using;
- Carefully mix in the whites and the diced apple;
- Pan fry with a bit of oil, turning 4 or 5 times as it cooks. They can be fried as individual pancakes. Serve warm with a dusting of icing sugar.

Opposite, papillotes, cocons de Lyon and coussins de Lyon, traditional sweets.

EGGS 'EN MEURETTE' WITH BEAUJOLAIS

Eggs, 1/2 litre of white Beaujolais, shallots, mushrooms, 1 head of garlic, meat rinds and fat, parsley stalks, 1 tbsp of flour, 1 tbsp of double cream, vinegar, 1 tbsp olive oil, bacon cut into cubes, diced tomatoes, toast rubbed with a little garlic.

Sauce:
Sweat the finely sliced shallots with the stalks from the mushrooms, one whole head of garlic, the meat and parsley stalks in some butter.
Add one spoonful of flour and the wine. Cook for thirty minutes.
Pass the sauce through a fine sieve and reduce it. Add the double cream. Keep warm.

Eggs:
Poach the eggs one by one in boiling water to which a little vinegar and a tbspoonful of olive oil have been added. The eggs will take between 3 and 4 minutes to cook.
Take the eggs out and dry them off on a clean towel. Dress them on some toasted bread which has been rubbed with garlic.
Pour the hot sauce over the eggs. Serve with mushrooms, bacon and diced tomatoes.

sweet. It is a cocoon-shaped sweet, composed of 40% marzipan, wrapped in a yellow paste made of praline, orange liqueur, cocoa butter and curaçao liqueur.

One last sweet can be noted, even if it has now disappeared. The 'pâté de vogue', was a hat-shaped pastry stuffed with pears macerated in alcohol. In Lyon, pregnant women would be described as having *'le ventre en pâté de vogue'* (a tummy like a pâté de vogue).

SMOOTH BEAUJOLAIS

The author Leon Daudet celebrated it as the *'troisième fleuve de Lyon'* (Lyon's third river), an inexhaustible flow which pours its hundreds of thousands of litres onto the world every year. Beaujolais is made with the Gamay grape, is drunk at cellar temperature and is quintessentially Lyonnais. It marries perfectly with any type of charcuterie, light meats, marinades and stronger, more characterful cheeses.

But Beaujolais is also a cooking wine which is used in many pork recipes: hot saucisson or sabodet with wine, or with *'gêne'* (young marc) or *'paradis'* (wine at the start of its fermentation). These delicacies are served at bistrots all over the region, as is andouillette *'marchand de vin'* (cooked in red or

An original Lyonnais vessel, 46 cc volume.

white wine), or eggs '*meurette*'. As far as fish is concerned, the pikeperch in red wine wins in popularity, closely followed by stuffed Dombes carp with white wine.

As for game and '*coq au vin*', the marinade is made with red or white wine, depending on the cook and his or her personal preference.

A festive wine if ever there was one, Beaujolais is on everyone's lips on the third Thursday in November, the traditional date of its annual launch. In Lyon, as all over the Beaujolais region, it is a time of celebration. It is incumbent on everybody to taste the Beaujolais nouveau, at the risk of wincing at its acidity. And the saying goes: '*le vrai, c'est encore ce qu'il y a de mieux !*' (true Beaujolais really is the best thing).

CONCLUSION

Lyon's history and geography have merged with the Lyonnais character, to make the antique capital of the Gauls the birth-place of superior gastronomical delights. Thus, with every century, Lyon became, with its Mères and its Bouchons and its regard for tradition, '*une ville de boit-sans-soif et de gourmets, de hume-piots et de torche-casseroles, de tire-à-boire et de lèche-grils*' (a town of inveterate drinkers and food-lovers, of pan-wipers and pot-sniffers, pump-fiends and griddle-lickers) as Marcel Grancher put it. Pierre Mérindol, the co-author of the first ever restaurant guide with Curnonsky, had a more qualified and admi-ring opinion: '*Un authentique Lyonnais à table, c'est, positivement, un régal pour les yeux*' (sitting opposite an authentic Lyonnais at a meal is a positively enchanting sight).

A conclusion could be chosen from Stendhal's writings, when he prophetically declares that: '*Aussi, tant qu'il demeurera un Lyonnais vivant, le flambeau gastronomique, bien que parfois agité par des vents contraires, continuera à répandre sa bienfaisante et lumineuse clarté sur le monde*' (As long as there is a Lyonnais alive on earth, the gastronomical flame will continue to spread its salutary light on all people, though often blown by contrary winds).

It is therefore not surprising that Lyon saw the Bocuse revolution in the mid-sixties. Nicknamed '*l'empereur des gueules*' (the foodies'emperor), he opened the way to a modern attitude to cooking which revisited the classical cuisine of previous generations and intro-duced a certain lightness and freedom in the preparations. His credo remained firm: respect for the produce. He was only 37 years old when he was awarded his third Michelin star and became the maestro of the French Nouvelle Cuisine which conquered the world. It is main-ly thanks to him that chefs have become the famous stars we know today.

Consecrated as the world ambassador of French Cuisine, he is also the originator of the '*journées gastronomiques*' in Lyon and of the most prestigious competition: the '*Bocuse d'Or*'.

A slight fog sometimes hovers over this town. For Henry Clos-Jouve, it was '*l'odoran-te et souple couronne formée au-dessus des deux collines par tous les fumets sortis des cas-seroles lyonnaises*': a fragrant and supple cloud, crowning the two hills, formed from the cooking vapours emanating from the saucepans all over Lyon.

BIBLIOGRAPHY

Benoit (Félix), *La cuisine Lyonnaise*, Ed. Solar, 1987;

Benoit (Félix), *Lyon Secret*, Ed. des Traboules, Brignais, 1993;

Brillat-Savarin (Anthelme), *Physiologie du Goût*, Ed. Flammarion, Paris, 1982;

Curnonsky et Grancher (Marcel), *Lyon, capitale mondiale de la gastronomie*, Ed. Lugdunum, Lyon, 1935, (Matagrin (Amédée), *Lyon, Cité des Brumes*, cité par Louis Maynard : *Anthologie de la capitale du bien-manger*, in);

Curnonsky, *Lyon capitale de la gastronomie*, revue Tourisme et vacances, 1947;

Etèvenaux (Jean), *La cuisine Lyonnaise*, Ed. La Taillanderie, Bourg-en-Bresse, 1996;

Fontaine (Jacques), *Recettes et Cuisines d'autrefois*, Ed. Horvath, Lyon, 1996;

Gambier (Gérald), *Cuisine Beaujolaise*, Ed. La Taillanderie, Châtillon-sur-Chalaronne, 1997;

Girard (Sylvie) et Valentin (Emmanuel et Christophe) (photos), *Cuisines régionales de France*, Le Lyonnais, Ed. du Fanal pour Ed. Time-Life, 1994;

Grison (Pierre) et Bay (Agathe) (photos), *Nouvelles Merveilles de la Cuisine Lyonnaise*, Ed. Xavier Lejeune, Lyon, 1996;

Grison (Pierre) et Lecoq (Philippe), *Les bouchons d'hier et d'aujourd'hui*, Ed. du Progrès, Chassieu, 1994;

Grison (Pierre), Bertinier (Jacques), Dubouillon (Alain), Redon (Jacky), *Les recettes des Authentiques Bouchons Lyonnais*, Ed. Rhône Imprim, Lyon, 1998;

Mesplède (Jean-François), *Saveurs de Lyon et du Rhône*, Ed. La Taillanderie, Bourg-en-Bresse, 1996;

Pitte (Jean-Robert), *Géographie historique et culturelle de l'Europe*, Presses Universitaires de Paris-Sorbonne, 1995;

Rabelais (François), *Pantagruel*, Ed. Pocket, Paris, 1998;

Rabelais (François), *Gargantua*, Ed. Pocket, Paris, 1998;

Rabelais (François), *Quart-Livre*, Ed. Pocket, Paris, 1998;

Selle (de la) (Hélène), *Cafés et Brasseries de Lyon*, Ed. Jeanne Laffitte, 1986,;

Stendhal (Beyle Henri dit), *Mémoires d'un touriste*, 1838, Ed. La Découverte, Paris, 1981;

Tendret (Lucien), *La table au pays de Brillat-Savarin*, Ed. du Bastion, Bourg-en-Bresse, 1986;

Varron (Marcus Ternetius Varro) (116-27 av. J.-C.), *Rerum Rusticarum Libri*, De Agricultura, traduction de Nisard.

Achevé d'imprimer en juin 2002
Dépôt légal 2ᵉ trimestre 2002
Printed in E.U., sur les presses de **beta**